This book belongs to

_____

_____

_____

_____

"

Treat your password like your toothbrush. Don't let anybody else use it, and get a new one every six months.

Website

Username

Password

Notes

Website

Username

Password

Notes

Website

Username

Password

Notes

Website

Username

Password

Notes

Website

Username

Password

Notes

Website

Username

Password

Notes

Website

Username

Password

Notes

Website

Username

Password

Notes

Website

Username

Password

Notes

Website

Username

Password

Notes

Website

Username

Password

Notes

Website

Username

Password

Notes

Website

Username

Password

Notes

Website

Username

Password

Notes

Website

Username

Password

Notes

Website

Username

Password

Notes

B

Website	
Username	
Password	
Notes	

Website	
Username	
Password	
Notes	

Website	
Username	
Password	
Notes	

Website	
Username	
Password	
Notes	

B

Website

Username

Password

Notes

Website

Username

Password

Notes

Website

Username

Password

Notes

Website

Username

Password

Notes

B

Website

Username

Password

Notes

Website

Username

Password

Notes

Website

Username

Password

Notes

Website

Username

Password

Notes

B

Website

Username

Password

Notes

Website

Username

Password

Notes

Website

Username

Password

Notes

Website

Username

Password

Notes

Website

Username

Password

Notes

Website

Username

Password

Notes

Website

Username

Password

Notes

Website

Username

Password

Notes

Website

Username

Password

Notes

Website

Username

Password

Notes

Website

Username

Password

Notes

Website

Username

Password

Notes

C

Website

Username

Password

Notes

Website

Username

Password

Notes

Website

Username

Password

Notes

Website

Username

Password

Notes

Website

Username

Password

Notes

Website

Username

Password

Notes

Website

Username

Password

Notes

Website

Username

Password

Notes

D

Website

Username

Password

Notes

Website

Username

Password

Notes

Website

Username

Password

Notes

Website

Username

Password

Notes

D

Website

Username

Password

Notes

Website

Username

Password

Notes

Website

Username

Password

Notes

Website

Username

Password

Notes

D

Website

Username

Password

Notes

Website

Username

Password

Notes

Website

Username

Password

Notes

Website

Username

Password

Notes

D

Website

Username

Password

Notes

Website

Username

Password

Notes

Website

Username

Password

Notes

Website

Username

Password

Notes

E

Website

Username

Password

Notes

Website

Username

Password

Notes

Website

Username

Password

Notes

Website

Username

Password

Notes

Website

Username

Password

Notes

Website

Username

Password

Notes

Website

Username

Password

Notes

Website

Username

Password

Notes

Website

Username

Password

Notes

Website

Username

Password

Notes

Website

Username

Password

Notes

Website

Username

Password

Notes

E

Website

Username

Password

Notes

Website

Username

Password

Notes

Website

Username

Password

Notes

Website

Username

Password

Notes

E

Website

Username

Password

Notes

Website

Username

Password

Notes

Website

Username

Password

Notes

Website

Username

Password

Notes

F

Website

Username

Password

Notes

Website

Username

Password

Notes

Website

Username

Password

Notes

Website

Username

Password

Notes

F

Website	
Username	
Password	
Notes	

Website	
Username	
Password	
Notes	

Website	
Username	
Password	
Notes	

Website	
Username	
Password	
Notes	

Website

Username

Password

Notes

Website

Username

Password

Notes

Website

Username

Password

Notes

Website

Username

Password

Notes

Website

Username

Password

Notes

Website

Username

Password

Notes

Website

Username

Password

Notes

Website

Username

Password

Notes

Website

Username

Password

Notes

Website

Username

Password

Notes

Website

Username

Password

Notes

Website

Username

Password

Notes

G

Website	
Username	
Password	
Notes	

Website	
Username	
Password	
Notes	

Website	
Username	
Password	
Notes	

Website	
Username	
Password	
Notes	

Website

Username

Password

Notes

Website

Username

Password

Notes

Website

Username

Password

Notes

Website

Username

Password

Notes

Website

Username

Password

Notes

Website

Username

Password

Notes

Website

Username

Password

Notes

Website

Username

Password

Notes

Website

Username

Password

Notes

Website

Username

Password

Notes

Website

Username

Password

Notes

Website

Username

Password

Notes

H

Website

Username

Password

Notes

Website

Username

Password

Notes

Website

Username

Password

Notes

Website

Username

Password

Notes

Website

Username

Password

Notes

Website

Username

Password

Notes

Website

Username

Password

Notes

Website

Username

Password

Notes

Website

Username

Password

Notes

Website

Username

Password

Notes

Website

Username

Password

Notes

Website

Username

Password

Notes

Website

Username

Password

Notes

Website

Username

Password

Notes

Website

Username

Password

Notes

Website

Username

Password

Notes

I

Website	
Username	
Password	
Notes	

Website	
Username	
Password	
Notes	

Website	
Username	
Password	
Notes	

Website	
Username	
Password	
Notes	

Website

Username

Password

Notes

Website

Username

Password

Notes

Website

Username

Password

Notes

Website

Username

Password

Notes

Website

Username

Password

Notes

Website

Username

Password

Notes

Website

Username

Password

Notes

Website

Username

Password

Notes

J

Website

Username

Password

Notes

Website

Username

Password

Notes

Website

Username

Password

Notes

Website

Username

Password

Notes

Website	
Username	
Password	
Notes	

Website	
Username	
Password	
Notes	

Website	
Username	
Password	
Notes	

Website	
Username	
Password	
Notes	

♦J

Website

Username

Password

Notes

Website

Username

Password

Notes

Website

Username

Password

Notes

Website

Username

Password

Notes

J

Website

Username

Password

Notes

Website

Username

Password

Notes

Website

Username

Password

Notes

Website

Username

Password

Notes

Website

Username

Password

Notes

Website

Username

Password

Notes

Website

Username

Password

Notes

Website

Username

Password

Notes

Website

Username

Password

Notes

Website

Username

Password

Notes

Website

Username

Password

Notes

Website

Username

Password

Notes

Website

Username

Password

Notes

Website

Username

Password

Notes

Website

Username

Password

Notes

Website

Username

Password

Notes

Website

Username

Password

Notes

Website

Username

Password

Notes

Website

Username

Password

Notes

Website

Username

Password

Notes

Website

Username

Password

Notes

Website

Username

Password

Notes

Website

Username

Password

Notes

Website

Username

Password

Notes

L

Website	
Username	
Password	
Notes	

Website	
Username	
Password	
Notes	

Website	
Username	
Password	
Notes	

Website	
Username	
Password	
Notes	

Website

Username

Password

Notes

Website

Username

Password

Notes

Website

Username

Password

Notes

Website

Username

Password

Notes

Website

Username

Password

Notes

Website

Username

Password

Notes

Website

Username

Password

Notes

Website

Username

Password

Notes

Website

Username

Password

Notes

Website

Username

Password

Notes

Website

Username

Password

Notes

Website

Username

Password

Notes

Website

Username

Password

Notes

Website

Username

Password

Notes

Website

Username

Password

Notes

Website

Username

Password

Notes

Website

Username

Password

Notes

Website

Username

Password

Notes

Website

Username

Password

Notes

Website

Username

Password

Notes

Website

Username

Password

Notes

Website

Username

Password

Notes

Website

Username

Password

Notes

Website

Username

Password

Notes

Website

Username

Password

Notes

Website

Username

Password

Notes

Website

Username

Password

Notes

Website

Username

Password

Notes

Website

Username

Password

Notes

Website

Username

Password

Notes

Website

Username

Password

Notes

Website

Username

Password

Notes

Website

Username

Password

Notes

Website

Username

Password

Notes

Website

Username

Password

Notes

Website

Username

Password

Notes

N

Website	
Username	
Password	
Notes	

Website	
Username	
Password	
Notes	

Website	
Username	
Password	
Notes	

Website	
Username	
Password	
Notes	

Website

Username

Password

Notes

Website

Username

Password

Notes

Website

Username

Password

Notes

Website

Username

Password

Notes

O

Website

Username

Password

Notes

Website

Username

Password

Notes

Website

Username

Password

Notes

Website

Username

Password

Notes

Website

Username

Password

Notes

Website

Username

Password

Notes

Website

Username

Password

Notes

Website

Username

Password

Notes

Website

Username

Password

Notes

Website

Username

Password

Notes

Website

Username

Password

Notes

Website

Username

Password

Notes

Website

Username

Password

Notes

Website

Username

Password

Notes

Website

Username

Password

Notes

Website

Username

Password

Notes

Website

Username

Password

Notes

Website

Username

Password

Notes

Website

Username

Password

Notes

Website

Username

Password

Notes

Website

Username

Password

Notes

Website

Username

Password

Notes

Website

Username

Password

Notes

Website

Username

Password

Notes

Website

Username

Password

Notes

Website

Username

Password

Notes

Website

Username

Password

Notes

Website

Username

Password

Notes

Website

Username

Password

Notes

Website

Username

Password

Notes

Website

Username

Password

Notes

Website

Username

Password

Notes

Website

Username

Password

Notes

Website

Username

Password

Notes

Website

Username

Password

Notes

Website

Username

Password

Notes

Website

Username

Password

Notes

Website

Username

Password

Notes

Website

Username

Password

Notes

Website

Username

Password

Notes

Website

Username

Password

Notes

Website

Username

Password

Notes

Website

Username

Password

Notes

Website

Username

Password

Notes

Website

Username

Password

Notes

Website

Username

Password

Notes

Website

Username

Password

Notes

Website

Username

Password

Notes

Website

Username

Password

Notes

Website

Username

Password

Notes

Website

Username

Password

Notes

Website

Username

Password

Notes

Website

Username

Password

Notes

Website

Username

Password

Notes

Website

Username

Password

Notes

Website

Username

Password

Notes

Website

Username

Password

Notes

Website

Username

Password

Notes

Website

Username

Password

Notes

Website

Username

Password

Notes

Website

Username

Password

Notes

Website

Username

Password

Notes

Website

Username

Password

Notes

Website

Username

Password

Notes

Website

Username

Password

Notes

Website

Username

Password

Notes

Website

Username

Password

Notes

Website

Username

Password

Notes

Website

Username

Password

Notes

Website

Username

Password

Notes

Website

Username

Password

Notes

Website

Username

Password

Notes

Website	
Username	
Password	
Notes	

Website	
Username	
Password	
Notes	

Website	
Username	
Password	
Notes	

Website	
Username	
Password	
Notes	

Website

Username

Password

Notes

Website

Username

Password

Notes

Website

Username

Password

Notes

Website

Username

Password

Notes

Website

Username

Password

Notes

Website

Username

Password

Notes

Website

Username

Password

Notes

Website

Username

Password

Notes

Website

Username

Password

Notes

Website

Username

Password

Notes

Website

Username

Password

Notes

Website

Username

Password

Notes

Website

Username

Password

Notes

Website

Username

Password

Notes

Website

Username

Password

Notes

Website

Username

Password

Notes

Website

Username

Password

Notes

Website

Username

Password

Notes

Website

Username

Password

Notes

Website

Username

Password

Notes

Website

Username

Password

Notes

Website

Username

Password

Notes

Website

Username

Password

Notes

Website

Username

Password

Notes

Website

Username

Password

Notes

Website

Username

Password

Notes

Website

Username

Password

Notes

Website

Username

Password

Notes

Website

Username

Password

Notes

Website

Username

Password

Notes

Website

Username

Password

Notes

Website

Username

Password

Notes

Website

Username

Password

Notes

Website

Username

Password

Notes

Website

Username

Password

Notes

Website

Username

Password

Notes

Website	
Username	
Password	
Notes	

Website	
Username	
Password	
Notes	

Website	
Username	
Password	
Notes	

Website	
Username	
Password	
Notes	

Website

Username

Password

Notes

Website

Username

Password

Notes

Website

Username

Password

Notes

Website

Username

Password

Notes

Website

Username

Password

Notes

Website

Username

Password

Notes

Website

Username

Password

Notes

Website

Username

Password

Notes

Website

Username

Password

Notes

Website

Username

Password

Notes

Website

Username

Password

Notes

Website

Username

Password

Notes

Website

Username

Password

Notes

Website

Username

Password

Notes

Website

Username

Password

Notes

Website

Username

Password

Notes

Website

Username

Password

Notes

Website

Username

Password

Notes

Website

Username

Password

Notes

Website

Username

Password

Notes

Website

Username

Password

Notes

Website

Username

Password

Notes

Website

Username

Password

Notes

Website

Username

Password

Notes

Website

Username

Password

Notes

Website

Username

Password

Notes

Website

Username

Password

Notes

Website

Username

Password

Notes

Website	
Username	
Password	
Notes	

Website	
Username	
Password	
Notes	

Website	
Username	
Password	
Notes	

Website	
Username	
Password	
Notes	

Website

Username

Password

Notes

Website

Username

Password

Notes

Website

Username

Password

Notes

Website

Username

Password

Notes

X

Website

Username

Password

Notes

Website

Username

Password

Notes

Website

Username

Password

Notes

Website

Username

Password

Notes

Website

Username

Password

Notes

Website

Username

Password

Notes

Website

Username

Password

Notes

Website

Username

Password

Notes

Y

Website

Username

Password

Notes

Website

Username

Password

Notes

Website

Username

Password

Notes

Website

Username

Password

Notes

Website

Username

Password

Notes

Website

Username

Password

Notes

Website

Username

Password

Notes

Website

Username

Password

Notes

Y

Website

Username

Password

Notes

Website

Username

Password

Notes

Website

Username

Password

Notes

Website

Username

Password

Notes

Z

Website

Username

Password

Notes

Website

Username

Password

Notes

Website

Username

Password

Notes

Website

Username

Password

Notes

Website

Username

Password

Notes

Website

Username

Password

Notes

Website

Username

Password

Notes

Website

Username

Password

Notes

Z

Website

Username

Password

Notes

Website

Username

Password

Notes

Website

Username

Password

Notes

Website

Username

Password

Notes

Z

Website

Username

Password

Notes

Website

Username

Password

Notes

Website

Username

Password

Notes

Website

Username

Password

Notes

Website

Username

Password

Notes

Website

Username

Password

Notes

Website

Username

Password

Notes

Website

Username

Password

Notes

Z

Website

Username

Password

Notes

Website

Username

Password

Notes

Website

Username

Password

Notes

Website

Username

Password

Notes

Z

Website

Username

Password

Notes

Website

Username

Password

Notes

Website

Username

Password

Notes

Website

Username

Password

Notes

Made in the USA
Monee, IL
15 October 2023

44618215R00063